MAR 1 7 2014

STEM *trailblazer* BIOS

ASTROPHYSICIST AND SPACE ADVOCATE

NEIL DEGRASSE TYSON

MARNE VENTURA

Lerner Publications Company
Minneapolis

Lerner Publications Company
A division of Lerner Publishing Group, Inc.
241 First Avenue North
Minneapolis, MN 55401 U.S.A.

For reading levels and more information, look up this title at www.lernerbooks.com.

Content Consultant: David Arnett, Regents Professor, Steward Observatory, University of Arizona

Library of Congress Cataloging-in-Publication Data

Ventura, Marne.
   Astrophysicist and space advocate Neil deGrasse Tyson / by Marne Ventura.
      p.   cm. — (STEM trailblazer bios)
   Includes index.
   ISBN 978-1-4677-2461-6 (library binding : alkaline paper)
   ISBN 978-1-4677-2491-3 (eBook)
   1. Tyson, Neil deGrasse—Juvenile literature. 2. Astrophysicists—United States—Biography—Juvenile literature. 3. Astronautics—United States—Juvenile literature. 4. Universe—Juvenile literature. I. Title.
   QB460.72.T97V46 2014
   523.01092—dc23 [B]   2013026972

Manufactured in the United States of America
1 – PC – 12/31/13

The images in this book are used with the permission of: The images in this book are used with the permission of: © eddtoro/Shutterstock Images, p. 4; © EpicStockMedia/Shutterstock Images, p. 5; © iofoto/Shutterstock Images, p. 7; © Bryan Bedder/Getty Images, p. 8; © Deborah Feingold/Corbis, p. 11; Wikimedia Commons, p. 12; © Lennox McLendon/AP Images, p. 14; © jiawangkun/Shutterstock Images, p. 15; Susan Gerbic, p. 16; NASA/SDO/AIA, p. 19; © Andrew Brusso/Corbis, p. 20; © fluidworkshop/Shutterstock Images, p. 21; Jim Grossmann/NASA, p. 23; © Cindy Ord/Getty Images, p. 24; © Mike Lawrie/Getty Images, p. 25; © Paul Drinkwater/NBC/NBCU Photo Bank/Getty Images, p. 26

Front Cover: © FOX Image Collection/Getty Images.

Main body text set in Adrianna Regular 13/22. Typeface provided by Chank.

CONTENTS

Chapter 1

The Hayden Planetarium introduced Neil to the wonders of the universe.

DISCOVERING THE NIGHT SKY

The lights in the **planetarium** dimmed. Nine-year-old Neil sat in the darkness and stared up at the huge domed ceiling. The audience grew silent. A voice boomed, "We are now in the universe, and here are the stars."

It was Neil's first visit to the Hayden Planetarium in New York City. He had seen the night sky many times from his home in the Bronx. He had seen a few stars and the moon. But tonight was different. On the ceiling above him, he saw countless stars, planets, and constellations—groups of stars that form shapes.

Neil was amazed by what he saw on the planetarium's ceiling.

HAYDEN PLANETARIUM

The Hayden Planetarium is a part of the Rose Center for Earth and Space at the American Museum of Natural History in New York City. Inside is a large Space Theater with seating for 429 people. Visitors can view images of stars, planets, and galaxies projected on the large domed ceiling.

Not long after this, Neil and his family took a trip to Pennsylvania. Away from the lights of New York City, he was able to see the stars more clearly. He realized the stars he had seen on the planetarium ceiling were not just part of a show. They were real. He wanted to know more about them. Neil felt like the universe was calling him.

GROWING UP IN THE BRONX

Neil deGrasse Tyson was born on October 5, 1958, in New York. He grew up in the Bronx in New York City. Neil lived with his parents, his older brother, and his younger sister in a tall building called the Skyview Apartments.

The Bronx's bright city lights made it difficult for Neil to see the stars in the night sky without a telescope.

Neil has spent his life learning and teaching about the universe.

Neil went to public school. He was an average student. He never had a teacher tell him that he was the best in the class or that he was going to go far. In fact, his third-grade teacher wrote a note on his report card. She said Neil should be more serious about his schoolwork.

GETTING A BETTER LOOK

After the family trip to Pennsylvania, a friend lent Neil a pair of binoculars. Neil went to the roof of his building and looked at the night sky through the binoculars. He was amazed to see craters—large, bowl-shaped holes—on the moon. He wanted to see more. When he was eleven, his parents bought him a telescope.

Soon Neil wanted a bigger telescope to learn more about **astronomy**. But a more powerful telescope cost two hundred dollars. Neil's parents didn't have a lot of extra money. So Neil started a business walking dogs for people who lived in his building.

He walked several dogs three times a day. Most days, he earned five dollars. He saved his money until he had enough to pay for half of the telescope he wanted. His parents paid for the other half.

Neil didn't stop walking dogs. He earned more money to buy a camera. He wanted to take photos of the stars and the planets he saw. At the age of eleven, Neil decided he would become an **astrophysicist**.

TECH TALK

"What's fun about telescopes is that if you've never looked through one, and then you look through one for the first time, at the moon or at Saturn, it is astonishing. Saturn has rings! Oh my gosh, the moon has craters! Things you've heard about and read about—but to experience them yourself becomes a singular moment in your life. You are there in the universe. And you can't get enough of it."

—*Neil deGrasse Tyson*

From a young age, Tyson was determined to be an astrophysicist.

Chapter 2

Neil learned more about astronomy and physics at the Bronx High School of Science.

LEARNING ABOUT THE UNIVERSE

Neil learned more about the stars. In sixth grade, he took astronomy courses at the planetarium. He often took his telescope to the roof of his apartment to study the night sky. Sometimes police officers would come up to make sure everything was okay. They weren't used to seeing people using telescopes in the Bronx. They were curious. Neil helped them look through the lens. He pointed out Saturn's rings and talked about how pretty he thought they were.

When he was ready for high school, Neil chose the Bronx High School of Science. When he was fifteen, Neil went to space camp. He spent a month studying the stars and the planets. He worked with scientists and other young people. When he got back to New York, he gave a talk to fifty adults. He told them what he had learned. Neil's career as an astrophysicist had begun.

COLLEGE YEARS

Neil graduated from the Bronx High School of Science in 1976. He applied to Harvard University in Massachusetts and Cornell University in New York. He got a letter from Carl Sagan, a famous scientist who taught at Cornell. Sagan had his own television show. He had written many books about the cosmos, or the universe. Sagan told Neil he hoped the young man would choose Cornell. Although Neil chose Harvard, he never forgot Sagan's kindness.

Neil couldn't believe it when he received a personal letter from the famous scientist Carl Sagan.

Neil studied physics at Harvard. He graduated in 1980. Then he worked toward advanced degrees at the University of Texas in Austin and Columbia University in New York City. While he studied astronomy, he earned money by teaching and writing about astrophysics for *StarDate* magazine. In 1989, his first book about the universe was published. It was titled *Merlin's Tour of the Universe*. He got his doctorate, the highest level of college degree, in astrophysics in 1991.

Neil received his doctorate in astrophysics from Columbia University.

Tyson autographs one of his books, titled *Origins*.

MERLIN'S TOUR OF THE UNIVERSE

Tyson's first book, *Merlin's Tour of the Universe*, was published in 1989. In it, a made-up character named Merlin comes from the Andromeda Galaxy. He tells of his conversations with famous scientists of the past, such as Albert Einstein, and answers popular questions about astronomy.

BECOMING A ROLE MODEL

Neil deGrasse Tyson had grown up in a time when African Americans were not always treated fairly. Tyson wanted to help make the world a better place for African Americans. During high school and college, he was on a wrestling team. In college, one of the wrestlers on Tyson's team told him he should not become an astrophysicist. He thought Tyson should work to improve life for African Americans. This bothered Tyson. But he didn't stop studying astrophysics.

A few years later, there was a solar flare, or small explosion, on the sun. A television station asked Tyson to be on the news. He explained the solar flare to the public. Tyson watched himself on TV. He saw that he was helping make the world a better place for people. He was an expert on astrophysics. He was teaching the public about space. He was a role model for young scientists.

TECH TALK

"I had never before seen a black person interviewed on television for expertise that had nothing whatever to do with being black. You think about it, you've seen blacks—sure, they're entertainers and actors and athletes—but when you look at people brought onto television as experts, watching myself, that was the first time I had ever seen it."

—Neil deGrasse Tyson

Tyson explained a solar flare to the public during his first appearance on television in 1989.

Chapter 3

Tyson's hard work earned him the job of director and head scientist at the Hayden Planetarium.

WORKING FOR THE UNIVERSE

Tyson worked as a researcher after college. He studied how stars form. He learned more about how stars explode. He studied dwarf **galaxies**. He found new facts about the Milky Way. In 1995, he became the director of the Hayden

Planetarium. Tyson was now the head of the place where he first fell in love with the night sky.

PLUTO

In 1997 the Hayden Planetarium was nearly sixty years old. It needed to be rebuilt. Tyson was in charge of the new displays. He removed Pluto from a solar system model. Tyson argued that Pluto didn't belong with the other planets. It was smaller and made mostly of ice. Some astronomers and museum guests did not agree with Tyson's decision. They thought Pluto should stay.

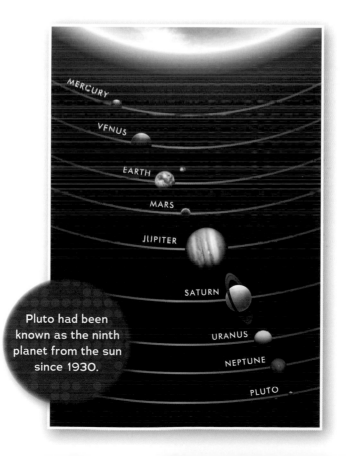

Pluto had been known as the ninth planet from the sun since 1930.

SPACE ADVOCATE

In 2001 and 2004, President George W. Bush asked Tyson for help. He wanted Tyson to work with other experts to study space exploration. Together they helped plan the US space program. Tyson became a space **advocate**. He wanted people to find out more about our universe. He thought everyone needed to understand science.

In 2006 the International Astronomical Union agreed with Tyson about Pluto. They named Pluto a dwarf planet. That same year, the National Aeronautics and Space Administration

From left:
Neil deGrasse Tyson, Bill Nye, Jim Bell, Scott Hubbard, and Louis Friedman, members of the Planetary Society board, pose at NASA's Kennedy Space Center in Florida in 2010.

(NASA) asked Tyson to join them. NASA had been formed the same year Tyson was born. When he was a boy, there were no African American astronauts, scientists, or engineers at NASA. He was glad to be a part of the space program.

Chapter 4

SATELLITE RADIO

Tyson shows off one of his cosmos vests during a visit to the SiriusXM Studios.

SHARING HIS LOVE FOR THE UNIVERSE

Tyson shows his love for the cosmos in many ways. He has a Saturn desk lamp in his office. He collects ties with cosmos on them. Tyson claims one of his ties is spaghetti-sauce-proof. If he spills food on it, it just looks like another

nebula! Tyson likes to wear his cosmic ties because it is like wearing the universe, he says. Since his first public talk at the age of fifteen, Tyson has found many ways to tell people about science.

BOOKS AND PAPERS

Tyson has written eleven books. He wants people who are not scientists to understand space and the universe. He wants them to enjoy it as he does. Tyson's autobiography is called *The Sky Is Not the Limit*. In it, he writes about growing up in the Bronx. He tells how he decided to become an astrophysicist. Tyson also writes for science magazines. And he writes papers about his research.

Tyson and comedian Eugene Mirman (*right*) answer science questions for a crowd in New York City in July 2011.

In 2009, Tyson appeared on *The Tonight Show* with Jay Leno.

TELEVISION

In 2004, Tyson was the host of a TV series called *Origins*. It told how life began. He was also the host of *NOVA ScienceNow* beginning in 2006. In this program, he made science news fun and easy to understand. Tyson has been a guest on many other TV shows.

RADIO

In the summer of 2009, Tyson created a radio talk show called *StarTalk*. He invites famous comedians to talk with him about science. By adding humor to science, he makes it fun for all people to learn more about astronomy and physics.

TWITTER

Tyson is active on Twitter, the social network where people tweet by posting short messages. So many people enjoy reading Tyson's tweets about the world of science that he won an award from *Time* magazine for having one of the top 140 Twitter feeds in the world in 2011 and 2012.

THE PLUTO FILES

After the International Astronomical Union stated that Pluto was no longer considered a planet, many people did not agree. They still wanted Pluto to be called a planet. On the TV show *The Pluto Files*, which aired in December 2011, Tyson traveled across the United States to find out why people were so passionate about Pluto.

AND BEYOND . . .

In May 2013, the Fox Network announced that Tyson is working on a television series called *Cosmos: A Space-Time Odyssey.* It will be a new way for Tyson to help people learn more about astrophysics.

TECH TALK

"I'd like to believe that the scientific literacy of the public can be . . . enhanced . . . by using the universe as a hook to get people interested in science. You just show them [how beautiful the universe is] and they'll say, 'I want to learn more.'"

—*Neil deGrasse Tyson*

TIMELINE

1958
Neil deGrasse Tyson is born on October 5 in New York City.

1976
Tyson graduates from the Bronx High School of Science in June.

1980
Tyson graduates from Harvard University and earns a degree in physics.

1991
Tyson earns a doctorate degree from Columbia University in astrophysics.

1995
Tyson becomes the director of the Hayden Planetarium.

2001
President George W. Bush asks Tyson to study the future of exploring space for the United States.

2006
Tyson begins hosting the first of five seasons of *NOVA ScienceNow*.

2009
Tyson creates and hosts the *StarTalk* radio talk show.

2011
Time magazine honors Tyson's Twitter feed as one of the top 140 in the world for the first time.

2013
In May, Tyson begins working on a television series called *Cosmos: A Space-Time Odyssey*.

GLOSSARY

advocate
someone who supports
an idea

astronomy
the study of stars, planets,
and space

astrophysicist
someone who studies the
physical properties of stars,
planets, and space

galaxies
large groups of stars
and planets

nebula
huge, bright clouds of gas or
dust in deep space

planetarium
a building with equipment
to project the positions and
movements of stars, planets,
the sun, and the moon onto a
dome-shape ceiling

SOURCE NOTES

10 Neil deGrasse Tyson, "When I Look Up," The Secret Life of Scientists
and Engineers, *Nova*, video, 2:21, accessed July 19, 2013, http://www
.pbs.org/wgbh/nova/secretlife/scientists/neil-degrasse-tyson.

18 Neil deGrasse Tyson, interview by Steve Curwood, "Reach for the
Stars," *Living on Earth*, MP3 audio, October 8, 2004, http://www.loe
.org/shows/segments.html?programID=04-P13-00041&segmentID=1.

22 Neil deGrasse Tyson, "30 Second Science," The Secret Life of
Scientists and Engineers, *Nova*, video, 0:46, accessed July 19, 2013,
http://www.pbs.org/wgbh/nova/secretlife/scientists
/neil-degrasse-tyson.

28 Neil deGrasse Tyson, interview by Steve Curwood, "Reach for the
Stars," *Living on Earth*, MP3 audio, October 8, 2004, http://www.loe
.org/shows/segments.html?programID=04-P13-00041&segmentID=1.

FURTHER
INFORMATION

BOOKS

Aguilar, David A. *13 Planets: The Latest View of the Solar System.* Washington, DC: National Geographic, 2011. Read about Pluto, four other dwarf planets, and the eight planets of our solar system.

Kops, Deborah. *Exploring Exoplanets.* Minneapolis: Lerner Publications, 2012. Find out how scientists detect planets far outside of our own solar system!

Waxman, Laura Hamilton. *Exploring Space Travel.* Minneapolis: Lerner Publications, 2011. Learn what it takes to get into outer space and what being in space is like for astronauts.

WEBSITES

NASA
http://www.nasa.gov/audience/forstudents/index.html
Read stories and play games about space!

NASA Lunar Science Institute
http://lunarscience.nasa.gov/articles
/the-most-astounding-fact-neil-degrasse-tyson
Find out what Neil deGrasse Tyson thinks is the most astounding fact about the universe!

PBS *NOVA: The Secret Life of Scientists & Engineers*
http://www.pbs.org/wgbh/nova/secretlife/scientists
/neil-degrasse-tyson
Watch and listen to Neil deGrasse Tyson speak about his first interests in the universe.

INDEX

ABOUT THE AUTHOR

Marne Ventura writes educational material for children in kindergarten to sixth grade. She has helped create more than fifty educational software products and apps for math, science, reading, and social studies. She lives with her husband on the central coast of California.